PERFORMANCE APPRAISAL OF SELECTED SHOPPING MALLS IN GUJARAT

:: Author ::

Dr. Chirag Raval

(M.Com., M.Phil, Ph.D.)

PUBLISHED BY

The New ERa International Publishing House
HQ. At & Po. Chaveli., Ta- Chansma,
Dist- Patan, North Gujarat, India, Asia.
www.iphouseindia.com

First Publication: 8th March, 2015

Copyright: Author
(c) **Dr. Chirag Raval**

ISBN:- 978-15-08949-77-0

Price: Rs.750/- INDIA
$ 15 OUTSIDE INDIA

PUBLISHED BY

The New ERa International Publishing House
HQ. At & Po. Chaveli., Ta- Chansma,
Dist- Patan, North Gujarat, India, Asia.
www.iphouseindia.com

INDEX

PREFACE

The retail scenario in India is unique. Development of shopping Malls in India is adding new dimensions to the booming retail sector. The Mall culture is really gripping the Indian consumers because of more awareness, recent trends and changing lifestyles. The Mall culture is catching up gradually in cities with several Malls making their entry in Gujarat retail sector.

The retail marketers try to understand the needs of different consumers and having understood his different behaviors which require an in depth study of their internal and external environment, they formulate their plans for marketing. When everything revolves round the customer, then the study of consumer behavior becomes a necessity. The study of consumer behavior is the study of how individuals make decisions to spend their available resources on consumption of related items. Mall culture is catching on fast in India. It has become the way of shopping in metros and tier I cities. Shopping malls of international scale and quality are expected to come up. Malls growth is being seen as a clear indicator of the economic prosperity in India. Significantly, the number of Malls in the country has increased at a fast pace. And they are doing brisk business. A trip to the local Mall will bear this out. So, I opted the shopping malls from selected cities of Gujarat state for my research work.

The study would be helpful in highlighting the role of shopping malls in development and services provided to consumers. This study helps to shopping malls towards the consumer's behavior and then they implement in their organization. The study helps to acquire a clear picture of national as well as state efforts to deal with the performance of shopping malls.

ACKNOWLEDGEMENT

First of all, I am very much grateful to God, He has given me ability, so I have completed my studies not only B.Com. but M. Com. and M.Phil. too. Now I am submitting thesis for award of Ph.D. Degree in Commerce.

A successful completion of a research work, especially of Ph.D. calls for intellectual nourishment, valuable guidance and professional help, selfless cooperation, encouragement, support and blessings from God.

I am deeply indebted and wish to express my sincere gratitude to my "Guruji" Dr. Pinakin R. Sheth, Associate Professor, Post Graduate Department of Business Studies, Sardar Patel University, VallabhVidyanagar, for his invaluable guidance, encouragement, critical comments and constant inspiration throughout the course of this investigation.

I am grateful to Dr. P.K.Rathod, Professor and Head, Former Head Dr. M.K.Patel P.G. Department of Business Studies, Sardar Patel University, VallabhVidyanagar for providing me assistance, support and guidance.

I express my gratitude to my Sir for extending their support for my research work, especially from Prof. Dr. S.K. Bhatt for his continuous support.

I am thankful to all faculty members of P.G. Department of Business Studies, Sardar Patel University, VallabhVidyanagar for guiding me through various stages of my research. I am also thankful to teaching and administrative staff of the P.G. Department of Business Studies.

I express my sincere thanks to Dr.Ketaki.P.Sheth for kind support and motivation throughout my work.

I am also thankful to Librarians of various institutions like IIMA, EDII, Bhaikaka Library, Gujarat University,

Nirma University, Gujarat Vidyapith, L.D. Engineering College etc.

I express a deep sense of gratitude towards the management of malls and my respondents who have helped me and co-operated me in doing this huge difficult work and provided me data in time.

I will be failing in my duty if I do not acknowledge my deep indebtedness to my parents Vasudevbhai and mother Sumitraben for their encouragement, support and blessings without which this study would not have been possible.

I acknowledge wholehearted support from my elder brother, Dr. Rajendra V. Raval, Gita bhabhi, niece Shivani and Prancy and elder brother Mr. KalpeshRaval, Poonambhabhi, nephew Vraj for giving valuable inputs.

I acknowledge the patience and assistance of my wife Kavita deserves appreciation for many lost hours of her convictable association with me during my study time when this research work occupied my attention and free time.

I acknowledge wholehearted support from my friends, Mr. Mahesh R. Prajapati and Mr. Gaurang C. Barot, Mr. KamleshVaghela, Mr. Ashwin Patel for giving valuable inputs.

Thus, any research work is result of combination of efforts and assistance of many well wishers to the investigator. This list is almost incomplete and I am grateful to all those who have helped me directly and indirectly in my research work.

Finally thanks do not see enough to the almighty to whom I owe everything.

Chirag V. Raval

CHAPTER-1

INTRODUCTION

Introduction

"Gujarat seeks to drive economic development balanced carefully with social development. The state aspires to benchmark itself with global economic powers on more than one attribute, such as Governance, Infrastructure and Human Development. Gujarat foresees itself as the numerouno state, leading the way for a prosperous India."

Gujarat has witnessed impressive industrial development since its formation as an independent state in 1960. The industrial sector at present comprises of over 1200 large industries and over 3,12,000 micro, smalland medium industries. As per the results of the Annual Survey of Industry (ASI), 2004-05 carried out by the Central Statistical Organization (CSO), under Ministry of Statistics and Programme Implementation, Government of India, Gujarat accounts for 17.2% of fixed capital investment, 15.6% of value of production and 13.7% of value added in industrial sector in India. Gujarat has achieved the distinction of being the top most industrially developed state in India in respect of investment in industrial sector and second among states in respect of value of production and value addition in industrial sector in India.

Today human needs have become more sophisticated and complex in nature and at the same time there are umpteen numbers of firms who see great opportunity for business potential and the intensity of battle for space has become very significant. This has given rise to marketing activities which are essentially marketing plans and programs with a view to countering competition and at the same time retain the business. The marketing activity has been in the business for long but it was not recognized as an organized function and an organized activity very crucial to the growth of an organization.

The Marketing plays a pivotal role in the growth and development of a country irrespective of a country irrespective of size, population and the concepts are so interlinked that, in the absence of one, another virtually cannot survive. It is a historical fact that the development of marketing has always kept pace with the economic growth of the country. Both have experienced evolutionary rather than revolutionary change. The objective of modern marketing is to make profits through satisfying consumer's needs and wants.

Consumer Behavior

All of us are consumers. We consume things of daily use; we also consume and buy these products according to our needs, preferences and buying power. These can be consumable goods, durable goods, specialty goods or, industrial goods.

What we buy, how we buy, where and when we buy, in how much quantity we buy depends on our perception, self-concept, social and cultural background and our age and family cycle, our attitudes, beliefs values, motivation, personality, social class and many other factors that are both internal and external to us. While buying, we also consider whether to buy or not to buy and from which source or seller to buy. In some societies there is a lot of affluence and, these societies can afford to buy in greater quantities and at shorter intervals. In poor societies, the consumer can rarely meet his barest needs.

The marketers therefore try to understand the needs of different consumers and having understood his different behaviors which require an in depth study of their internal and external environment, they formulate their plans for marketing.

Management is the youngest of sciences and oldest of arts and consumer behavior in management is a very young discipline.

The study of consumer behavior is the study of how individuals make decisions to spend their available resources on consumption of related items. It includes the study of what, why, how, when, where they buy and how often they buy any particular product or service. Consumer behavior is the act of individuals in obtaining and using goods and services which are exhibited through their decision process consumer purchases are likely to be influenced by physiological and sociological and sociological factors.

Definition of Consumer Behavior

Consumer behavior can be defined as the decision making process and physical activity involved in acquiring, evaluating, using and disposing of goods and services.

This definition clearly brings out that it is not just the buying of goods / services that receives attention in consumer behavior but, the process starts much before the goods have been acquired or bought. A process of buying starts in the minds of the consumer, which leads to the finding of alternatives between products that can be acquired with their relative advantages and disadvantages. This leads to internal and external research. Then follows a process of decision making for purchase and using the goods, and then the post purchase behavior which is also very important because it gives a clue to the marketers whether his product has been a success or not.

To understand the likes and dislikes of the consumer, extensive consumer research studies are being conducted. These researchers try to find out.

- What the consumer thinks of the company's products and those of its competitors?
- How can the product be improved in their opinion?
- How the customers use the product?
- What is the customer's attitude towards the product and its advertising?
- What is the role of customer in his family?

Performance Appraisal

Performance appraisal indicates the level of desired performance level, level of actual performance and the gap between these two. This gap should be bridged through personnel department techniques like training, executive development etc. A unit/organization's objectives can be achieved only when people/employees put in their best efforts. How to ascertain whether an employee has shown his/her best performance on a given job? The answer is performance appraisal. A performance appraisal is a process of evaluating an employee's performance of a job in terms of its requirements. In fact performance appraisal is the basis for personnel department. It was viewed that performance appraisal was useful to decide upon employee promotion, transfer, demotion, termination, salary determination and the like.

Definitions:

(1) Scott, Clothier and Spiegel. "Merit rating is the process of evaluating the employee's performance on the job in terms of the requirements of the job."

(2) In the words of Dale Yoder, 'The term personnel appraisal refers to the formal procedures used in working organizations to evaluate the personalities and contributions and potential of group members.'

Objectives of Performance Appraisal:

McGregor Says, 'Formal performance appraisal plans are designed to meet three needs, one for the organization and the other two of the individual. They are as follows:

➤ They provide systematic judgment to back up salary increases, transfers, demotions or terminations.

➤ They are means of telling a subordinate how he is doing and suggesting needed changes in his behavior, attitudes, skills or job knowledge.

➤ They are used as a base for coaching and counseling the individual by the superior.

If put in details, they are used for following purposes: (1) Promotion, (2) Transfer, (3) Training and development, (4) Wage and salary administration, (5) Personnel Research and (6) Self improvement.

Some of the Significant Features of Performance Appraisal may be captured thus:

➤ Performance appraisal is the systematic description of an employee's job-relevant strengths and weaknesses.

➤ The basic purpose is to find out how well the employee is performing the job and establish a plan of improvement.

➤ Appraisals are arranged periodically according to a definite plan.

➤ Performance appraisal is not job evaluation. It refers to how well someone is doing the assigned job. Job evaluation determines how much a job is worth to the organization and, therefore, what range of pay should be assigned to the job.

➤ Performance appraisal is a continuous process in every large scale organization.

➤ Employee's ability and skill are evaluated in it.

➤ It is a search of employee's strengths and weaknesses.

➤ The appraisal is done by the supervisor or by somebody conversant with the employee.

About Gujarat

Gujarat is recognized as one of the leading industrial states in India, augmenting the growth of the services sector and leading to immense prosperity for its people. The state's manufacturing sector has been instrumental in its growth and development, with the smalland medium enterprise (SME) sector playing a key role in shaping the manufacturing industry.

Gems & Jewellery is one of the fastest growing sectors in the country. The state of Gujarat has the distinction of being the world's second largest producer of gold jewellery, contributing the highest share (85 per cent) to the total national jewellery production. With eight out of 10 diamonds in the world being polished in Surat, it is known as the 'Diamond Capital of the World' having the world's largest diamond processing hub with a 72 per cent world share and 80 per cent of the Indian market.

GUJARAT AT A GLANCE:

Geographical Area	1,96,024 sq.km (6.19% of India)
Capital	Gandhinagar
Districts	26

Population	50 million (5% of India)
Languages	Gujarati, Hindi and English
GDP (at current price)	US$ 45.3 billion
Per Capita Income (at current price)	US$ 915
Urbanization rate	38 % (vis-a-vis India's 28%)
Per Capita Power Consumption	1,354 units (National Average : 665)
Cellular Connection	41 per 1000 persons (National Average : 26)
Motor Vehicles	118 per 1000 persons (National Average: 57)
Percentage of State Population to all India Population	4.93
National Highway Length	1572 Km.

Road Length	74,018 km-95% surfaced road.
Railway	5188 km (8.25% of India)
Ports	42
Industrial Zone and Parks	263
International Air Port (Ahmedabad)	01
Domestic Airports	13 (Ahmedabad, Vadodara, Surat, Rajkot, Bhavnagar, Bhuj, Mandvi, Mundra, Jamnagar, Kandla, Keshod, Porbandar, Palanpur)

(GUJARAT AT A GLANCE)

Selected cities of Gujarat:

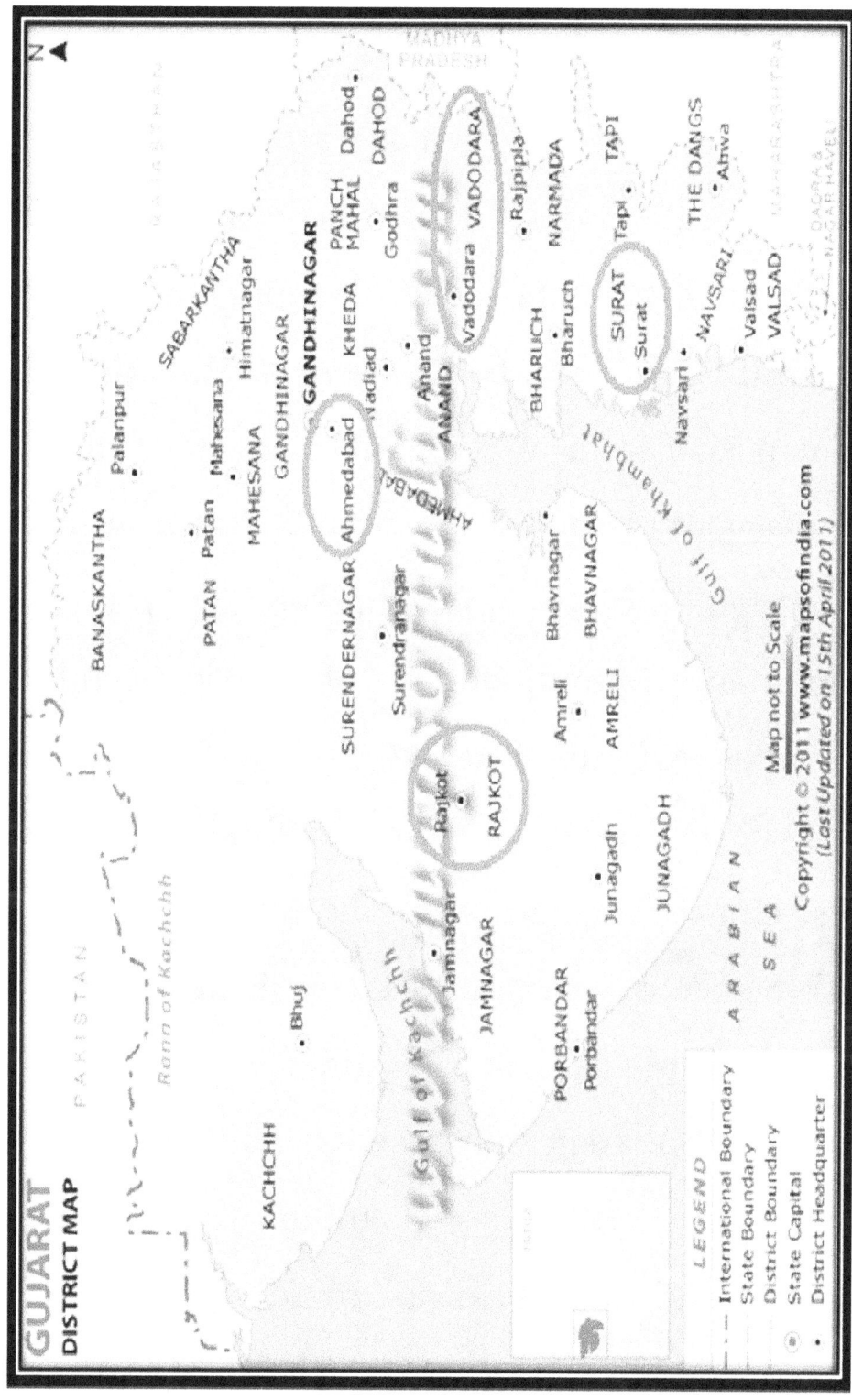

Profile of Selected Cities and Malls:

Ahmedabad:

Ahmedabad also known as Karnavati, is the largest city in Gujarat, India. It is the former capital of Gujarat and is also the judicial capital of Gujarat as the Gujarat High Court has its seat in Ahmedabad. It is also financial capital of Gujarat. It is the fifth largest city and seventh largest metropolitan area of India, with a city population of approximately 5.6 million and metropolitan population of 6.4 million. In 2010, Forbes magazine rated Ahmedabad as the fastest-growing city in India, and third in the world after two Chinese cities — Chengdu and Chongqing.

Ahmedabad was founded on February 26, 1411 by Sultan Ahmed Shah to serve as the capital of the Gujarat Sultanate, and was named after him. Under British rule, a military cantonment was established and the city infrastructure was modernized and expanded. In first episode of this series 'Ahmedabad is changing', how malls, supermarkets, hypermarkets and chains of retail stores altogether are changing Ahmedabad city and the people of Ahmedabad. Malls are as follow:

- Big Bazar malls near Iscon temple and at City pulse multiplex(Ten acre)in Raypur area, Ahmedabad.
- TATA's Star Bazar , Satellite road, Ahmedabad
- TATA's lifestyle superstore 'Westside' Mithakhali area, Ahmedabad
- Pantaloons' lifestyle superstore at Mithakhali area and Ten acre mall (Raypur)
- V – Mart stores at Law Garden and at Fun republic
- Vishal supermarket at SG highway and JunaShardamandir-Law Garden road
- 10 Acres, Opposite Arya Samaj Mandir, Ahmedabad
- Galaxy Super Mall, 23, Harekrishna Complex, Near Cadila Crossing, ,Ahmedabad.
- **Pyramid Mall:** A very popular and leading mall in Ahmedabad, Pyramid Mall consists of number of stores and shops of many domestic and

international brands. Near ParimalGarden,Ellisbridge, Ahmedabad - 380 006

- **Himalaya Mall :**A centrally air conditioned mall, it is situated in prime location of the city. It has stores of all the major brands related to clothes men & women, shoes, accessories etc. Near Indraprastha Tower,Drive In Road, Memnagar, Ahmedabad - 380 052

- **R3 The Mall:** A premier shopping and leisure destination in the city, it is one of the upcoming malls in the city which houses about 200 shops, food courts and a multiplex. ,Opp. ManavMandir, Nr. Mayflower Women's Hospital, Memnagar, Ahmedabad-380052.

- **Iscon Mall :** One of the famous and popular malls in the city, it comprises all the famous international and domestic brands in categories of garments, electronics, cosmetics, accessories, shoes etc under one roof. Satellite, Polytechnic, Ahmedabad –

380 015.

- **Parsvnath Mall:** A fabulous life style destination, Parsvnath Mall is a shopping mall cum multiplex. Where you can do shopping in various branded store and can watch movies as well. Vastrapur, Ahmedabad - 380 015;

- **Gallops Mall:** A newly built mall in Ahmedabad, it is built over 3.46 lakh square feet which consists of a small multiplex of about 76 seat capacity apart from the stores of leading domestic and international brands., S G Highway, B/H Iscon Temple, Satellite Area, Ahmedabad - 380 015.

- **APM Shopping Mall:** Yet another Mall in the area, APM features a number of branded stores like Arrow, Louis, Philppe, Levi's, Lee and many more.Shyamal Char Rasta, Satellite, Ahmedabad - 380 015

Vadodara:

Vadodara formerly known as Baroda, is the third most populated city in the Indian State of Gujarat. It is one of four cities with a population of over

1,200,000million. Historical and archaeological findings date this place back to the 9th century when it was a smalltown called Ankottaka (present Akota) located on the right bank of the river Vishvamitri (whose name is derived from the great saint Rishi Vishwamitra). Ankottaka was a famous centre of Jainism in the 5th and 6th century AD. Some of the Akota bronze images can be seen in the Vadodara Museum. The city was once called Chandanavati after its ruler Raja Chandan of Dor tribe of Rajputs, who wrested it from the Jains. The capital had also another name "Virakshetra" or "Virawati" (a land of warriors). Later on it was known as Vadpatraka or Wadodará, which according to tradition is a corrupt form of the Sanskrit word Vatodar means 'in the heart of the banyan tree'. It is now almost impossible to ascertain when the various changes in the name were made; but early English travellers and merchants mention the town as Brodera, and it is from this that the name Baroda is derived. Again in 1974 the name changed to Vadodara.

Vadodara is the third most populated city in the Indian state of Gujarat after Ahmedabad and Surat. It is one of four cities in the state with a population of over 1 million, the other being Rajkot. It is also known as the Sayaji Nagari (Sayaji's City after its famous ruler, Maharaja Sayajirao Gaekwad III) or Sanskari Nagari (The City of Culture, a reference to its status as the Cultural Capital of Gujarat). Vadodara or Baroda, formerly the capital city of the Gaekwar State, is situated on the banks of the Vishwamitri, a river whose name derived from the great saint Rishi Vishwamitra. It is located southeast of Ahmedabad, 139 km from state capital, Gandhinagar. It is the administrative head quarters of Vadodara District. Both the railway line and national highway connecting Delhi and Mumbai, passes through Vadodara.

In line with the 'Knowledge City' vision of the Confederation of Indian Industry, Vadodara is gradually becoming a hub in Gujarat for IT and other development projects.Vadodara is also home to the Vadodara Stock Exchange (VSE). Malls are as follow:

Inox Leisure Ltd : Road No-21, GopalBaug, Gotri, Vadodara, Gujarat 390021 - 0265 2386600

Subhiksha Trading Service Ltd : Sb 1 To 5 Alien Complex Near Navdeep Complex, Nizampura, Vadodara, Gujarat 390002

Adani Enterprises Limited : 402, Duruv Avenue, Shobhana Nagar Society, Vasna Road, Vadodara, Gujarat 390015

Centre Square Mall, Vadodara, Gujarat.

Surat:

Surat also known as Suryapur, is the commercial capital city in state of Gujarat. Surat is India's eighth most populous city and ninth-most populous urban agglomeration. It is also administrative capital of Surat district and one of the fastest growing cities in India. The city proper is the third cleanest city in India. Surat is Gujarat's second largest city with a population of 4.5 million. Surat ranks fourth in a global study of fastest developing cities conducted by the city Mayors

Foundation,an international think tank on urban affairs. It is the fastest growing Indian cityin terms of economic prosperity. The city is located 306 km south of state capital Gandhinagar, and is situated on the left bank of the Tapti River (Tapi), the centre being around 22 km (14 mi) from its mouth. A moat divides the older parts of the city, with its narrow streets and handsome houses, and the newer suburbs. The city is largely recognised for its textile and diamond businesses. It is also known as the diamond capital of the world and the textile capital/Manchester textile city of India, a distinction it took over from Ahmedabad. It is also known as the "Embroidery capital of India" with the highest number of embroidery machines than any other city.92% of the world's diamonds are cut and polished in Surat. It has one of the highest GDP growth rates in India at 11.5% as of 2008.Surat was the primary port of India during the Mughal period, a distinction it lost to Bombay during the British Raj.

Malls are as follow.

City Mall : Abhushan Complex, GhodDhod Road, Parle Point, Surat, 395007

Regency Exclusive Ratail Shop : Opposite MinaraMasij, Baranpuri, Bhagal, Surat, 395003

Iscon Mall : Dumas Road, Subhash Nagar, Gujarat 395007 - 0261 3990444

Raj Empire Mall : Fame Raj Empire, Raj Empire Mall, Bhatar Road, Surat, Gujarat 395002 - 0261 2239999

Supreme - The IT Mall : Ring Rd, Sanjay Nagar, Surat, Surat, Gujarat 395002 - 0261 3993000

Big Bazaar Mall : SubhashNagar, Surat, Gujarat

Surat shopping is enjoyed by the customers as they can choose from a variety of products. There are a number of shopping centers in Surat to shop from. The city has always remained an important trading center from ancient times. With the progress of time, the city has been highly commercialized.

Rajkot:

Rajkot is the 4th largest city in the state of Gujarat, India. Rajkot is the 28th urban agglomeration inIndia, with a population more than 1.43 million as on 2008.Rajkot is ranked 22nd in The world's fastest growing cities and urban areas from 2006 to 2020.

Rajkot is a city of Gujarat state in India and administrative headquarters of the Rajkot District, 245 km from the state capital Gandhinagar, located on the banks of the Aji River and Nyari River. Rajkot was the capital of the then Saurashtra state from 15 April 1948 to 31 October 1956 before merging in bilingual Bombay State on 1 November 1956. Rajkot was merged into Gujarat State from bilingual Bombay state on May 1, 1960.

Once upon a time Rajkot was the hub of India in the field of Diesel engine and submersible Pumps. Still, Submersible pumps are manufactured in a lot and marketed throughout India and some of the big manufacturers also export them. Malls are as follow.

Cinemax and Grand Central Mall,"Cinemax is good cinema with 3 screen but rates are still high, people will prefer to go far to complex for reasonable price"

Crystal Mall, Rajkot, Gujarat

Brain Storm Shopping Mall,NN C House, Amin Marg, Rajkot, Gujarat 360002.

The Mall culture is catching up gradually in cities with several Malls making their entry in Gujarat retail sector.

CHAPTER- 2
RESEARCH METHODOLOGY

Research Methodology

The research methodology is used for collection, analysis and tabulation of data for the research. The selected tools are being utilized for the particular research, following is the detailed design used in the research.

Rationale of the study

A study focuses on performance appraisal of selected shopping malls in Gujarat. The study would be helpful in knowing the performance appraisal of selected shopping malls. The study would be highlighting the consumer behavior towards shopping malls in Gujarat.

Scope of the study

Shopping malls of international scale and quality are expected to come up. Malls growth is being seen as a clear indicator of the economic prosperity in India. Significantly, the number of Malls in the country has increased at a fast pace. And they are doing brisk business. A trip to the local Mall (there will be one in every locality soon!) will bear this out. So, I opted the shopping malls from selected cities, viz; Ahmedabad, Vadodara, Surat and Rajkot cities of Gujarat state for my research work.

Objectives of the study

The research study has been based on certain objectives. The specific objectives of present study are as follows:

- To evaluate overall performance of shopping malls and the customers' perception regarding service quality

- To identify the factors influencing the consumer behavior while selecting shopping Malls.

- To extract the source of information through which, consumer come to know about various shopping Malls.

- To identify problems faced by consumer while purchasing through shopping Malls.

- To know customers' expectations from shopping malls.

- To know the facilities provided to the consumers by the shopping Malls.

Hypotheses of the study

The present study has the following hypothesis to be proved subject to the objectives of the study.

- There is significant relation between the facilities provided by shopping malls and customer satisfaction.

- Shopping malls do not perform all promotion activities.

- Consumers have similar problems while purchasing through shopping Malls.

- There are large gaps between customers' expectations from shopping malls and services provided by shopping malls.

Research Design

The study is descriptive research study in nature The purpose of descriptive surveys, according to Ezeani (1998), is to collect detailed and factual information that describes an existing phenomenon. The descriptive research attempts to describe in detail the relationship between various aspects of a research problem. The major emphasis will be given to description of the state of affairs as exists at present. The study is divided into various stages such as objectives, methods of data collection and selection of sample size.

Sources of data

In order to achieve the objectives of the present study, there are two types of data collection methods. 1. Primary data 2. Secondary data.

1. Primary data

The primary data was collected from consumers of selected cities of Gujarat through interviews, personal investigation, visits etc. The necessary information on area of the study from shopping mall organization and consumers of selected cities. While collecting the data every care was taken to maintain its objectivity and accuracy.

Questionnaire

A separate questionnaire was prepared for consumers and Management of Shopping Malls to obtain the necessary feedback and data. Consumers and

Management of Shopping Malls were interviewed and requested to answer the questionnaire. A structured questionnaire was used to collect the primary data. A modified pre-tested questionnaire was used for the collection of data on the study. All questions of the questionnaire were put as a close-ended. The questionnaire was specifically designed to accomplish the objectives of the study.

2. Secondary data

Secondary data was collected from published literature on area of the study. Published literature such as reference books, national and international journals, magazines, newspapers, websites and other published sources were utilized to collect relevant and useful secondary data.

Sampling Plan

➢ **Sampling Unit:** The target population of the study was visitors in malls of Gujarat. A census of eight malls from four cities of Gujarat was taken. Shopping malls and consumers of particular shopping malls from selected cities of Gujarat. Each shopping mall is treated as a separate entity.

➤ **Sample size:** The total sample size consists of four cities of Gujarat such as Ahmedabad, Vadodara, Surat, and Rajkot of Gujarat state. Out of which a sample of two hundred forty (240) consumers and sixteen (16) selected shopping malls has been taken from the selected cities of Gujarat.

The total sample size taken for the present study was 240 (60 from each city). The distribution of selected respondents is given as below :

(Mall wise break-out)

Mall	No. of respondents
Baroda Centre	15
Big Bazaar	75
D-Mart	28
Himalaya	16
Iscon Mall	22

MORE	23
Reliance Mall	39
Seven Seas	22
Total	**240**

(City wise break-out)

City	No. of respondents	No. of Malls
Ahmedabad	60	04
Rajkot	60	04
Surat	60	04
Vadodara	60	04
Total	**240**	**16**

Out of these 240 respondents, 92 (38.3%) were married, 108 (45.0%) were unmarried while others were engaged, widow, separated or deserted. Their age ranges from 17-49 years, with a mean age of 27.21 years. The academic qualifications of the participants were classified in to following groups:

- Primary

- Higher Secondary

- Graduate

- Post Graduate and higher

Sampling Method: A two stage random sampling technique was used to select 240 respondents. At first stage, malls were randomly selected from each city. At second stage, from selected malls, pre-decided number (60) of visitors was selected using "Simple Random Sampling".

Samples are based on selected cities such as Ahmedabad, Vadodara, Surat, and Rajkot of Gujarat state.

Procedure:

The researcher traveled to all four cities, selected in the study and administered the instrument to respondents (visitors) after their oral concern. Following the instructions on the instrument, the questionnaires were filled and returned.

Data Analysis Plan

The data are edited, coded and classified. In order to make the collected data self speaking, interesting and more clear, they are analyzed in the form of tables, diagrams and graphs. Statistical techniques like percentage, mode, mean and medium analysis are used to analyze the data properly to get fair view regarding various aspects of study.

Frequency tables and cross tables were prepared with graphical presentation. Descriptive statistics was also obtained when it required. Pearson Chi – Square test was employed to check association between two attributes. The data analysis was carried out with the help of statistical software "SPSS" (Student Version). For each statistical test, corresponding p – values were obtained and on the basis of this value, the last conclusion for rejection / acceptance of the particular hypothesis was made. The researcher had put the level of significance (l.o.s.) at 5%. i.e. if the p-value was less than 0.05, null hypothesis was rejected otherwise accepted.

Significance of the study

The present study is quite significant due to the fact that this would be the study regarding the performance appraisal of selected shopping malls. The study would be helpful in highlighting the role of shopping malls in development and services provided to consumers. This study helps to shopping malls towards the consumer's behavior and then they implement in their organization.

The study helps to acquire a clear picture of national as well as state efforts to deal with the performance of shopping malls.

Limitations of the study

As every coin has two sides, the research study also has two sides there are certain limitations, which deceive the objects of the study. The study is conducted at selected shopping malls of selected cities of Gujarat state and hence is valid for Gujarat state only. The sample size is prefixed for the research study. Although the study will do with limitations it is definitely a pointer towards certain trends which could be used as basis for more extensive research effort of a similar nature.

CHAPTER- 3
REVIEW OF LITERATURE

Researchers, Scholars, Teachers, Academicians, Students, Practitioners, Industrial Association, Government and non government organizations etc are making a conscious study of literature through discussing keeping themselves alert to needs timely. In the present study also, before examining 'Performance appraisal of selected shopping malls in Gujarat' it is necessary to review the literature on the subject. The purpose of referring the research paper, project reports, articles, website and working it also provides supportive drive and evidence for the findings of the study. A number of studies have been conducted in the world, India and Gujarat which examined the subject. Following is just an indicative list of such literature –

- Meyer tries to bring out the importance of first impressions in selecting retail outlet by a customer. He discusses as to how first impression is formed and how a successful retailer can use this knowledge to his or her advantage.

(Meyer, G.Warren, Harris, G.Edward.,Kohns, P.Donald., and stone III, R.James. Retail Marketing, 8th edition, Mc-graw Hill international, Singapore – 1988.)

- In one of the chapters entitled "the retailing revolution", Davison, et.al., highlights the origin and the decades of changes that has taken place in global retailing since the end of world war II and thereafter. He says that change is now a constant factor in retailing. Almost any social, economic or political event of consequence will affect how consumers decide and behave in the market place. Retailers must recognize charge, adapt to it, and prosper from it if not, their competitors most surely will.

(Davidson, R. William., Sweeney J. Daniel, and Stampfl, W.Ronald, Retailing Management, John Wiley & Sons, USA, 1988.)

- Walters investigates the impact of retail price promotions on consumer purchasing patterns and the performance of competing retailers.

  (Walters G. Rockney, "Assessing the impact of retail price, promotions on product substitution, complementary purchase and interstore sales displacement", Journal of Marketing, Vol. 55, No.2, April 1991, p.17-29.)

- Devasahayam gives us the main reasons why customers normally do not shift loyalties from the small retailer to supermarkets in this study.

  (Devasahayam, Madona "A big Dea", Praxis – Business Line's Journal on Management, Vol. 2, No. 2, August 1998.)

- To document the changes in retail environment from its early days, the ETTG report volume I had conducted a comprehensive study of the Indian retailing environment. It brings out the current business status and its potential in India, as well as the practices and management philosophy on all key facts of retail business, like the retail consumers, different retail formats, retail location, and customer management and so on.

(Economic times intelligence group report, Retail, 1st edition, Economic times, 2000, 11.)

- Today shoppers want the total customer experience: superior solutions to their needs, respect, an emotional connection, fair price and convenience. Berry in his article brings out five pillars for the success of any retail business.

(Bery, B.Leonard, "The old pillars of new retailing" Harvard business Review, April 2001, p.131-137.)

- While customers should feel they are getting the most efficient service, employees on the other hand need to be highly motivated and have a fulfilled experience at work. Wold[5] in her article gives ten tactics to boost morale of the employees working in the retail outlet.

(Wold, Barbara "Retail your customers and staff" Images retail, Vol. No. 2, January 2003, p.42.)

- Kaushesh analysis the trends of past and present retailing and illustrates how the past can provide a road map for the present retailers. It explains several strategies used by different retailers – ranging from the traditional strategy based on low price and convenience to the recent strategies based on value, customer relationship and customer experience. It also helps in identifying the most suitable mix of strategies for present retailers.

  (Kaushesh, Anshul. "Retailing: The way forward" Marketing mastermind, April 2004, p.41-46.)

- The report prepared by business world provides insights on an overview of India, consumer psychographics, about retail in India and Asia and also retail and consumer trends in Asia and India in specific.

(The marketing white book: the essential hand book for Marketers, Business World, 2nd Edition, 2005.)

- Barbara finds customers top ten sales and customer service requirements in her study.

   (Wold, Barbara "Retain your customers and staff" images retail, vol. 16 – July 15, 2005, p.26-27.)

- Lusch, et.al., in one of the chapters "understanding the retail customers", discuses about the retail patronage model. It is a process model, moving from left to right. The process begins when the consumer recognizes a need to shop. The consumer then evaluates shopping alternatives and selects a store or stores to visit. Each store as it is visited is continuously evaluated so the consumer can decide whether study in the store and shop or leave. The consumer will reach closure if offerings in the store are favorably evaluated. Finally we move to the outcomes stage, in which the consumer purchases, postpones purchases, and does additional searching, or decides not to buy. Consumer is continuously storing information for future use in shopping situations and therefore, the model has a feedback loop. In addition each stage of the model is affected by the information sources that continually bombarded the consumer.

(Lysch, F. Robert, Dunne Patrick, and Gable, Myron, Op. Cit.)

- ZameerAsif in his paper has discussed Mall Management and has concluded that mall Management has emerged as the single most differentiating factor in today's scenario where the numbers of malls are multiplying. The need of the malls to differentiate themselves is a sure way of emerging winner and this positioning is ensured through Mall Management.

(ZameerAsif "Management of Events/Promotion at DLF city center Mall, Gurgaon" Indian Retail Review Vol. 1, Issue 1, January 2007).

- Venkateshwarlu H finds organized retailing globally, Retail industry – GDP and employment and FDI in Indian retailing opportunities and threats in his study.

(Venkateshwaralu H. and Ranjanic.v. "FDI in retailing A boon or a bane?" The Indian Journal of commerce, Vol. 60, No.1, January – March - 2007, p.1-9.)

- Sinha Piyushkumar and Kar Sanjay Kumar conducted research study to identify and classify the different formats of retailing in India. The study classifies the different formats of retailing in different categories and also explains the growth of each category and motivation of retailers to expand in to specific category. Most of organized retailers in India are harping on quality, service, convenience, satisfaction and assured benefits to shoppers in to the store. Consumer is the focus of retail business and the retailers should serve the consumer better, faster and less cost.

(Sinha Piyushkumar and Kar Sanjay Kumar "An insight in to the growth of new retail formats in India", IIM-A, 03-04 March, 2007)

- Dey tries to bring out growth of retailing and limitation and challenges in retailing in the study.

   (DeyDipankar, "GAIs and Transnational Retailing – few concerns and challenges". The ICFAI Journal of Management Research, Vol. 6, No. 6, 2007, p.63-76.)

- Anbalagan tries to bring out the growth of retail consumer market, opportunities, emerging trends in retail consumer marketing and reason for the change in the Indian consumer in the study.

   (Anbalagan M.A. Gunasekaram V., "Retail Consumers market in India – the next big leap" Indian Journal of Marketing, Vol. 37, No.3, March – 2007, p.24-29.)

- Devdeep gives us the idea focus on Mall bubble and what's the lack of Indian Mall in his study.

   (Singh Devdeep, SoniAditi "The Mall bubble" 4Ps – Business and Marketing, Vol. II, Issue. 11, 6th July – 19th July 2007, p.95-99.)

- Srivastava investigates retail situation in India as well as global perspective and international entries in Indian retail and also gives suggestions to retailers and government for improvement in her study.

(SrivastavaRuchi and SrivastavaBinkey. "Retail its global perspective" synergy. Journal of I.T. & Management, Vols. No. 2, July 2007, p.108-115.)

- Gupta Anupama investigates retailing human resources challenges ahead and FDI in retail sectors in her study.

(Gupta Anupama, "Retailing Human Resource Challenges Ahead" Synergy – 1.7 S Journal of I.T. & Management, Vol. 5, No.2, July 2007, p.12-107.)

- KureshiSonal, SoodVandana, Koshy Abraham conducted a research study on "Comprehensive Analysis of Exclusive brand store Customer in Indian Market". The objective of the research was to provide insight about the profile of the consumers of exclusive brand store, based on their demographic and psychographic characteristics. The findings of the research are as follows: 73.9 percent of the customers who visited the store were males. Three-fourths males belonged to the age group of 21-30. This clearly indicated that there was an under representation of women customers and people in the age group of 40 years. Majority of the customers coming to the store were students (33%) and young executives working in the private sector belonging to affluent households with income above 4.5 lakhs.

(KureshiSonal, SoodVandana, Koshy Abraham, "Comprehensive Analysis of Exclusive brand store Customer in Indian Market", IIM-A, 02nd August, 2007, 2007-08.)

- The article published in Indian Journal of Marketing provides insights on impact of Mall on retail trade, the reasons for retail Boom in twin cities, reasons for slow adoption of Malls.

(Venkateshwarlu H., Rajani C.V., "SMallVs Mall" – Indian Journal of Marketing, Vol. 37, No.10, October 2007, p.29-33.)

- Singla Amit and Goyal Anilkumar provided excellent description on the Indian retail industry in their paper entitled "The Retail Industry: From Myth to Malls". The paper discusses in detail the growth drivers for retail industry, investment opportunities in different sectors of retailing with high growth potential and fastest growing formats. After analyzing the retail industry, author concluded that the organized retail has opportunities to grow in India in spite of the kirana stores.

(SinglaAmit and GoyalAnilkumar, "The retail Industry: From Myth to Malls" published in Indianmba.com).

- Dash Prakash Chandra studied and explodes the opportunities , challenges and strategies of Indian retail sectors. The paper discusses the challenges like merchandising mix, retail differentiation, supply chain management and also competition from supplier's brand in Indian perspective.

(Dash Prakash Chandra "Indianretai Industry-Opportunities, Challenges and Strategies" published in www.indianmba.com).

- Baseer gives us the prospects and problems of Indian retailing trends in Indian retailing industry and the biggest problem of retail outlets in his study.

  (BaseerAmatal, LaxmiPrabta G. "Prospects and problems of Indian Retailing" – Indian journal of Marketing, Vol. 37, No. 10, October, 2007, p.26-28.)

- Malliswari investigates the emerging trends and strategies in Indian retailing and growth of hypermarkets and Malls in the study.

  (Malliswari M.N. "Emerging trends and strategies in Indian Retailing Indian Journal of Marketing vol. 37, No. 11, November – 2007, p.21-27.)

- Shah A.D. conducted a research study on " A study of Consumer Behaviour in Malls Vis-à-vis Mom & Pop Shops". This research has made it possible to understand the comparative consumer behavior at greater depth specifically with reference to behavior in malls and in mom and pop shops.

(Shah A.D. conducted a research study on " A study of Consumer Behaviour in Malls Vis-à-vis Mom & Pop Shops", September 2009).

- Kuruvilla Shelja Jose in his case study has briefly touched on HR practices in Malls in Mumbai. The author has suggested that Malls in India literally have a blank sheet of paper on which to create a new HR function.He tries to understand the challenges faced by Mall Management in fulfilling the HR function when areas as cleaning and security have been contracted out.

    (Kuruvilla Shelja Jose "The River side Mall- A case study" published in Synthesis, Vol 4, No.2, December 2007).

- Kainth Gurusharan Singh and Joshi Divakar studied the perception of customer & retailers towards Malls in Jalandhar in Punjab. The study was undertaken to learn about peoples' knowledge, beliefs, preferences and satisfaction. Most of consumer agreed that professional Mall Management and wide range of cheaper product have persuaded them to spend more time and money at Mall.

(Kainth Gurusharan Singh and Joshi Divakar "The perception of customer & retailers towards Malls in Jalandhar in Punjab, published in www.indianmba.com, 2008).

CHAPTER- 4

MANAGEMENT OFSHOPPING MALLS

Mall culture is catching on fast in India. It has become the way of shopping in metros and tier I cities. How this phenomenon is spreading fast in tier II cities as well. Small tier III cities will also be gripped by this Mall culture in future.

The Mall culture is really gripping the Indian consumers because of more awareness, recent trends and changing lifestyles.

Mall would provide suitable environment, particularly to the age group of 15 to 45 for shopping. Indian retail boom is evident even in smaller towns and cities of the country where organized retail formats have increasingly become popular. Development of mega Malls in India is adding new dimensions to the booming retail sector.

The word retail is derived from the French word 'retailer', meaning to cut a piece of or to break bulk. In simple terms, it implies a firsthand transaction with the customer.

The word 'Retail' is derived from a French ford with the prefix 're' and the verb 'trailer' meaning "to cut again". Thus, retail trade is one that cuts off smaller portions from large lumps of goods. It is a process through which goods are transported to final consumers. It consists of the all activities involved in selling, renting and providing goods and services to ultimate customers for personal, family and household use.

Retailing is an important marketing activity. Not only do producers and consumers meet through retailing actions, but retailing also creates customer value & has a significant impact on the economy.

To consumer, the value of retailing is in the form of utilities provided. Retailing's economic value is represented by the people employed in retailing as well as by the total amount of money exchanged in retail sales,

Meaning of Retail, Retailer and Retailing

Some definition can be given to clearly explain the meaning of retail retailer & retailing.

1. Retail

"Sale of goods to the public in small quantities." - Oxford Dictionary.

2. Retailer

Business whose sales come primarily from retailing. - Philip Kotler& Armstrong.

3. Retailing

Retailing includes all activities incident to selling to the ultimate consumers. - American Definition Committee.

4. Retailing

Retailing is selling final consumer products to householders. - McCarthy.

5. Retailing

"All Activities involved in selling goods or services directly to final consumer for their personal, non-business use." - Philip Kotler& Armstrong.

6. Retail

David Gilbert has defined retail as any business that

directs it marketing efforts towards satisfying the final consumer based upon the organization of selling goods and services as a means of distribution.

7. Retailing

Retailing can be referred to all the activities involved in the marketing and distribution of goods and services.

Retailing in India

Indian grocers were perhaps among the first in the world to acquire professional retailing skills. There is the old story of a good retail grocer and the bad retail grocer in India.

Once upon a time there were two grocers. One was perceived to be good and the other was considered bad. The good one always used to weigh his cereals, pulses, grams, etc. in such a way that if had to weight a kilogram he would initially place in the weighing balance produce less than a kilogram and then keep adding to it until it reached the required weighed. The bad retailer, on the other hand, always rather unconsciously placed much more and then kept removing stuff from the scales until it weighed a kilogram. The good retailer had actually acquired such skills to create a positive image in the minds of the customers.

Long ago, the **father of the nation, Mahatma Gandhi** realized the importance of the customer for the retailer; he is in fact the first to emphasize on the importance of customer relationship management practices in India. What he said about the importance of the customer is famous the world over. It goes like this: **"The customer is the most important person on our premises."**

- ✓ He is not dependent on us, we are dependent on him.
- ✓ He is not an interruption of our work; he is the purpose of it.
- ✓ He is not an outsider on our business, he is part of it.
- ✓ We are not doing him a favour by serving him,
- ✓ He is doing us a favour by giving us the opportunity to do so."

Key Trends in Urban India:

- Retailing in India is witnessing a huge revamping exercise.

- Estimated to be US$ 200 billion, of which organized retailing (i.e. modern trade) makes up 3 percent or US$ 6.4 billion.

- India is rated the fifth most attractive emerging retail market: a potential goldmine

- Ranked second in a Global Retail Development Index of 30 developing countries drawn up by AT Kearney.

- India is rated the fifth most attractive emerging retail market: a potential goldmine

- Food and apparel retailing key drivers of growth.

- Organized retailing in India has been largely an urban phenomenon with affluent classes and growing number of double-income households.

Key Trends in Rural India:

Rural markets are emerging as a huge opportunity for retailers reflected in the share of the rural market across most categories of consumption

- ITC is experimenting with retailing through its e-Choupal and ChoupalSagar – rural hypermarkets.

Growth of organized retailing in India

Organized retailing in India initially began in the south. The availability of land at prime locations coupled with lower real estate pries made multi storied shopping complexes possible. And now south India – notably Chennai and, to a lesser extent Bangalore and Hyderabad has emerged as a centre of organized retailing.

It took two years of recession for this concept of shopping to take root in major cities like Mumbai and Delhi. Recession brought down property prices in these cities, and it was during this slump that big business houses took notice of the potential in retailing.

(Retail in South-East Asia)

Country	Traditional	Organized
India	98%	2%
China	80%	20%
South Korea	85%	15%
Indonesia	75%	25%
Philippines	65%	35%
Thailand	60%	40%
Malaysia	50%	50%

(Source: Crisil)

India is rapidly evolving into an exciting and competitive marketplace with potential target consumers in both the niche and middle class segments. Manufacturer owned and retail chain stores are springing up in urban areas to market consumer goods in a style similar to that of Malls in more affluent countries. Even though big retail chain like crossroads, Saga and Shoppers Stop are concentrating on the upper segment and selling products at higher prices, some like RPGs Food World and Big Bazaar are tapping the huge middle class population. During the past two years, there has been a tremendous amount of interest in the Indian retail trade from global majors as well. Over the years international brands like McDonalds, Swarovski, Lacoste, Domino's, Pepsi Benetton among a host of others have come in and thrived in India. Retailing is one of the fastest growing industries in India, catering to the world's second largest consumer market. A sunrise industry, it offer tremendous potential for growth and contributes 8-10% to overall employment. However, this is still low compared to 20% in the USA. As India moves towards being a service oriented economy, a rise in this percentage is expected. The number of the retail outlets is growing at about 8.5% annually in the urban areas, and in towns with a population between 100000 to 1 million the growth rate is about 4.5%. with the increasing assertiveness of the Indian consumer and a growing supply base – both from within India as well as from other countries the retail sector in India is poised for a significant change in the coming decade.

(Percentage of Organized Retail)

Country	Percentages
USA	85%
Taiwan	81%
Malaysia	55%
Thailand	40%
Brazil	36%
Indonesia	30%
Poland	20%
China	20%
India	3%

(Source: Crisil)

(Number of Malls in Major Cities of India)

Cities Name	2005	2007	2010
Other Cities	34	86	97
Hyderabad	8	16	23
Bangalore	8	20	27
Pune	11	23	32
Kolkata	10	20	31
Chennai	2	6	11

Mumbai, Navi Mumbai, Thane	36	71	96
Noida and Ghaziabad	15	29	42
Gurgon	13	34	47
Delhi	21	51	78
Total	158	356	484

(Source: Crisil)

According to this year's Global Retail Development Index India is positioned as the leading destination for retail investment. This followed from the saturation in western retail markets and we find big western retailers like Wal-Mart and Tesco entering in to India market. India's retail industry accounts for 10% of its GDP and 8% of the employment to reach $17 billion by 2010. There are about 300 new Malls, 1,500 supermarkets and 325 departmental stores being built in the cities very soon.

About the Mall

A Mall is the arrangement of retail stores and

providing the right mix of shopping, food courts and entertainment and parking facilities.

The retail space is shared by anchor stores and other retailer who pays the developers of the Mall rent or lease payment for putting up the shop within the Mall premises. For e.g. pyramid Mall, Himalaya Mall etc.

Several Malls are coming up at Gujarat. New Malls are cropping up and existing ones are permitting the city with new branches. The Mall culture is catching up gradually in city with several Malls making their entry in Gujarat retail sector. These Malls have given a new dimension to shopping experience. Malls have transformed once compulsive and sober shopping in to a family entertainment and as a weekend pastime. With the entire products available less than one complex, offering rich and pleasant ambience and stocking. Several big players of India and mega retailers of the world are choosing the city as their retail destination. During the last five years, the Ahmedabad city had witnessed the development of Malls, hypermarkets, spread of supermarkets in every nook and corner of the city and emergence of several specialty stores. The factors for this rapid growth of retail industry in the city are the city boost of highest number of upper income households, spending habits of the citizens, relatively low real estate costs, and low risk of return ratio. The competition among retailers has become very stiff. Retailers are widening their coverage area, crossing borders and shattering cultural barriers. Technological changes are playing a pivotal role in retail industry in providing better services and reduction in overhead costs.

The Mall is complete shopping experience with the availability at choices, so many brands, impeccable ambience and food under one single roof.Malls provide not only a great ambiance but shopping, entertainment and F&B options under one single roof.

Biggest Malls of India

Name	Place	Area (Sq. feet)	Parking	Unit

Mantri Square	Banglore	919516	2080	202
Ambience Mall	Gudgaon	873000	2500	165
Great India	Noida	850000	5500	190
RCT	Mumbai	657000	3000	165
High Street	Mumbai	650000	3939	165

(Source: Sandesh, Thursday, 22nd April 2010)

Biggest Malls of World

Name	Place	Area (Sq. feet)	Parking	Unit
Dubai	UAE	3770000	14000	1200
West Admonton	Canada	3400000	20000	900
Barjaya Time	Malaysia	3400000	1000	-
Mall Off	America	3074000	12550	520
Jirscity	Philipines	3000000	4000	800

(Source: Sandesh, Thursday, 22nd April 2010)

Indian retail sector has undergone a complete transformation in recent times. For a long time, the corner grocery store was the only choice available to the consumer, especially in urban areas. From supermarkets and hypermarkets, to department stores and convenience stores and one stop shops, a retailing wave is currently sweeping the country.

CHAPTER- 5

ANALYSIS AND INTERPRETATION OF DATA

5.1: Consumer Behavior towards Shopping Malls:

Frequency Table

Distribution of respondents according to age group

Age group	Frequency	Percent
<25	84	35.0
25-30	76	31.7
31-35	60	25.0
>35	20	8.3
Total	240	100.0

Distribution of respondents according to gender

Gender	Frequency	Percent
Male	174	72.5
Female	66	27.5
Total	240	100.0

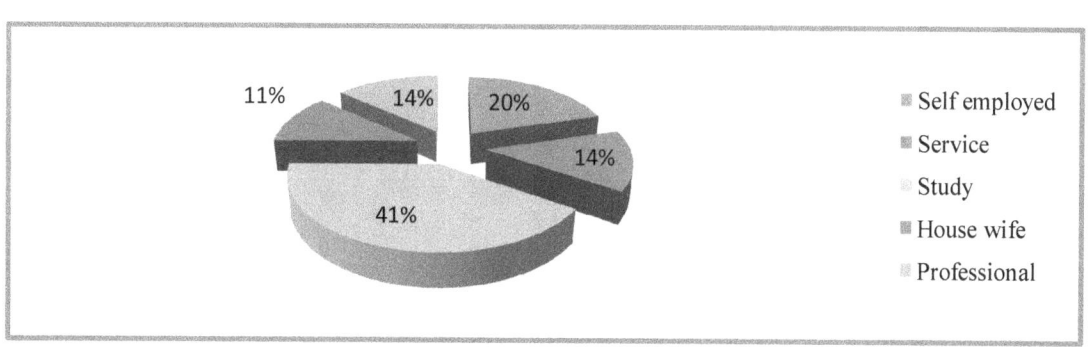

Distribution of respondents according to occupation

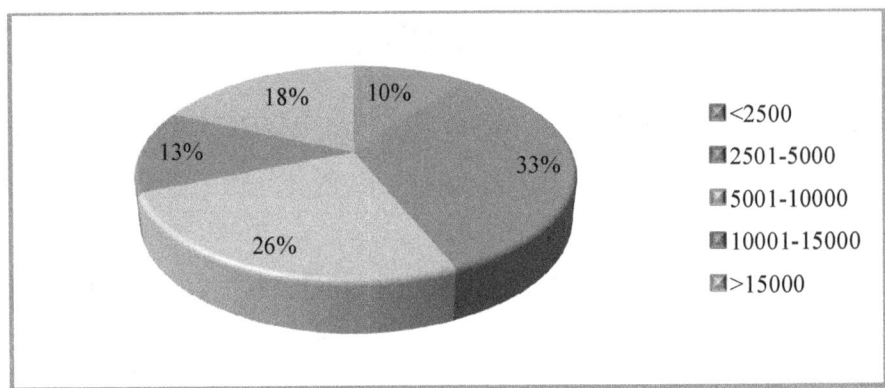

Distribution of respondents according to monthly income

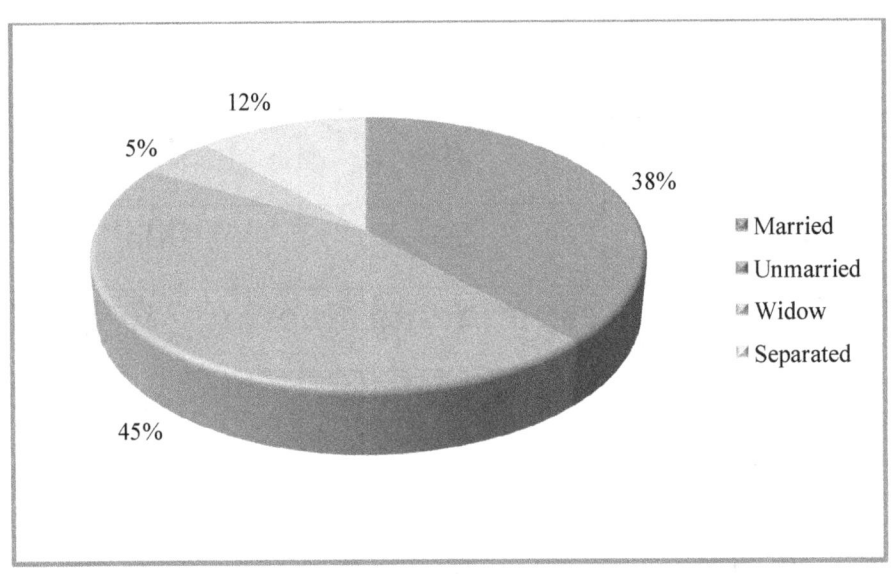

Distribution of respondents according to marital status

Distribution of respondents according to education

Education	Frequency	Percent
Uneducated	12	5.0
SSC	20	8.3
HSC	69	28.7

Graduate	62	25.8
Higher Education	77	32.1
Total	**240**	**100.0**

Distribution of respondents according to frequency of visit mall in a month

Frequency of visit a mall	Frequency	Percent
Once	49	20.4
Twice	24	10.0
Three	55	22.9
Fourth	30	12.5
Fifth	30	12.5
Sixth	52	21.7
Total	**240**	**100.0**

Distribution of respondents according to preferable time for visit mall

Preferable Time for Visit a Mall	Frequency	Percent

Morning	53	22.1
Afternoon	67	27.9
Evening	120	50.0
Total	**240**	**100.0**

Distribution of respondents according to preferable day for visit mall

Preferable Day for Visit a Mall	Frequency	Percent
Sunday	57	24
Monday	12	05
Tuesday	8	03
Wednesday	62	26
Thursday	21	09
Friday	3	01
Saturday	8	03
Any day	69	29
Total	**240**	**100.0**

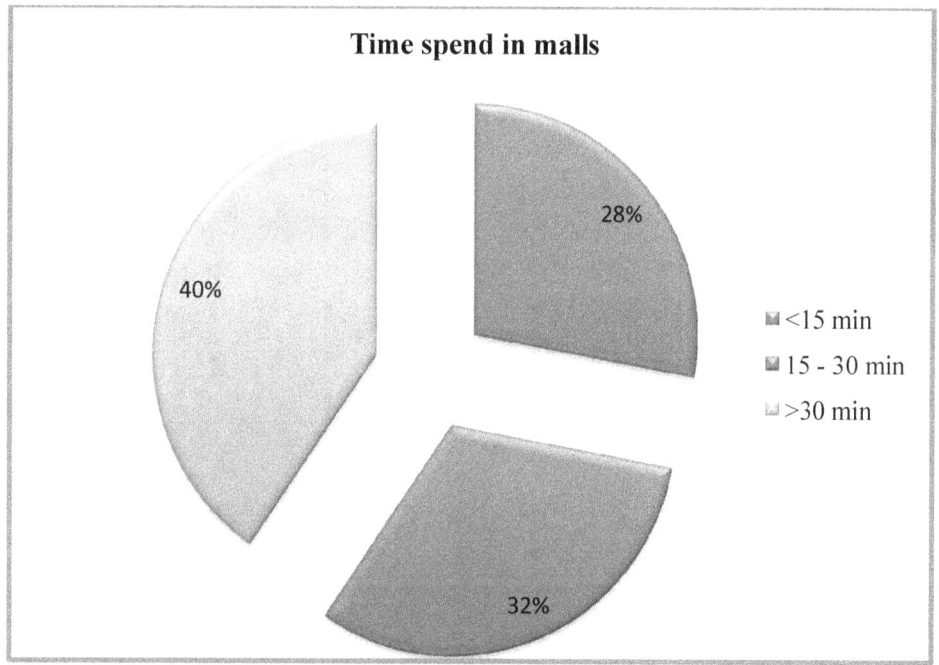

Distribution of respondents according to time spend in mall

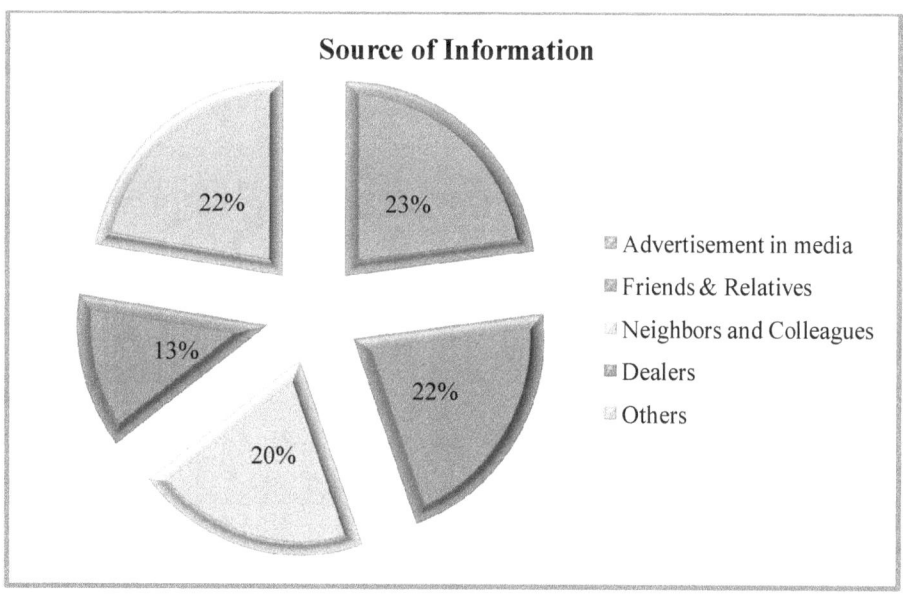

Getting information by consumers about various Malls

Decision maker for choice of mall

Decision Maker	Frequency	Percent
Self	81	33.8
Spouse	31	12.9
Family member	43	17.9
Friends	29	12.1
Relatives	38	15.8
Other	18	7.5
Total	**240**	**100.0**

Distribution of respondents according to city and mall

Mall	City				Total
	Ahmedabad	Rajkot	Surat	Vadodara	
Baroda Centre	0	0	0	15	**15**
Big Bazaar	31	26	18	0	**75**

D-Mart	0	13	15	0	**28**
Himalaya	16	0	0	0	**16**
Iscon Mall	0	11	11	0	**22**
MORE	0	0	0	23	**23**
Reliance Mall	13	10	16	0	**39**
Seven Seas	0	0	0	22	**22**
Total	60	60	60	60	**240**

Note: Now onwards each mall's name is abbreviated as follows.

Mall Original Name	Abbreviations
Baroda Centre	BC
Big Bazar	BB
D-Mart	DM
Himalaya	Him
Iscon Mall	ISC
MORE	MO
Reliance Mall	Rel

Seven Seas	SS

Views of respondents regarding facilities provided by different malls in selected cities

Facility	City			
	Ahmedabad	Rajkot	Surat	Vadodara
Store Atmosphere	Very Important	Very Important	Very Important	Very Important
Relaxation & Enjoyment	Important	Neutral	Neutral	Neutral
More Space to Move in	Neutral	Neutral	Very Important	Neutral
A Good Elevator System	Important	Very Important	Very Important	Important
Convenient Layout at the Mall	Very Important	Neutral	Very Important	Less Important
Easily Accessible Billing Counters	Very Important	Very Important	Very Important	Very Important
Trial rooms	Very Important	Very Important	Neutral	Very Important
Easily locatable stairs	Important	Neutral	Neutral	Neutral
Ample Parking Space	Important	Very Important	Important	Not Important
Prolonged Experience	Very Important	Neutral	Neutral	Neutral
Promotion Scheme	Very Important	Neutral	Very Important	Very Important

Table shows views of respondents regarding facilities provided by different malls in selected cities. As per majority of respondents, "Store atmosphere", "Easily accessible billing counters", "Promotion schemes" and "Trail rooms" are very important whereas for other facilities of malls, various respondents had mix opinion.

Views of respondents regarding facilities provided by different malls

Facility	Name of Mall							
	BC	BB	DM	Him	ISC	MO	Rel	SS
Store atmosphere	V IMP	V IMP	V IMP	V IMP	V IMP	V IMP	V IMP	V IMP
Relaxation & enjoyment	N	V IMP	N	V IMP	V IMP	N	N	N
More space to move in	V IMP	N	V IMP	N	N	N	Not IMP	N
A good elevator system	IMP	IMP	IMP	N	V IMP	Less IMP	V IMP	N
Convenient layout at the Mall	V IMP	V IMP	V IMP	V IMP	V IMP	Less IMP	N	V IMP
Easily accessible billing canters	V IMP	V IMP	V IMP	V IMP	V IMP	N	V IMP	IMP
Trial rooms	V	V	Less	V	V	V	N	V

	IMP	IMP	IMP	IMP	IMP	IMP		IMP
Easily locatable stairs	N	IMP	N	V IMP	N	N	N	N
Ample parking space	V IMP	V IMP	N	V IMP	IMP	Not IMP	V IMP	Less IMP
Prolonged experience	IMP	N	Less IMP	N	N	N	N	IMP
Promotion scheme	Not IMP	V IMP	Not IMP	V IMP	V IMP	N	Not IMP	V IMP

Table shows views of respondents regarding facilities provided by different malls. As per majority of respondents, "Store atmosphere", "Easily accessible billing counters", "Ample parking space" and "Trail rooms" are very important whereas for other facilities of malls, various respondents had mix opinion.

Frequency of purchasing various products from malls by respondents in selected cities

	City			
Product	**Ahmedabad**	**Rajkot**	**Surat**	**Vadodara**
Books	Sometimes	Sometimes	Sometimes	Sometimes
Grocery	Sometimes	Regularly	Regularly	Never
Food	Sometimes	Regularly	Regularly	Sometimes

Entertainment	Sometimes	Sometimes	Sometimes	Sometimes
Cosmetics	Sometimes	Regularly	Never	Regularly
Electronics	Sometimes	Never	Sometimes	Never
Furniture	Never	Regularly	Never	Sometimes
Home Decor	Sometimes	Never	Never	Sometimes
Clothes	Sometimes	Sometimes	Sometimes	Never

Above table presents frequency of purchasing various products from malls in selected cities. As per respondents of Rajkot and Surat city, majority were regularly purchasing Grocery, Food, Cosmetics and Clothes whereas respondents of Ahmedabad and Vadodara, majority was purchasing various products occasionally.

Frequency of purchasing various products from selected malls by respondents.

Product	Name of Mall							
	BC	BB	DM	Him	ISC	MO	Rel	SS
Books	Sometimes	Sometimes	Sometimes	Regularly	Sometimes	Regularly	Sometimes	Sometimes
Grocery	Never	Never	Regularly	Never	Regularly	Never	Regularly	Sometimes
Food	Some	Some	Regul	Regul	Regul	Regul	Regul	Regula

	times	times	arly	arly	arly	arly	arly	rly
Entertainment	Never	Sometimes	Sometimes	Sometimes	Sometimes	Sometimes	Sometimes	Sometimes
Cosmetics	Regularly	Sometimes	Regularly	Sometimes	Never	Regularly	Regularly	Regularly
Electronics	Sometimes	Never	Sometimes	Sometimes	Sometimes	Sometimes	Never	Regularly
Furniture	Never	Never	Sometimes	Regularly	Regularly	Regularly	Regularly	Sometimes
Home Decor	Sometimes	Sometimes	Never	Never	Sometimes	Sometimes	Never	Sometimes
Clothes	Regularly	Sometimes	Regularly	Regularly	Never	Regularly	Sometimes	Regularly

Above table presents frequency of purchasing various products from malls in selected cities. As per respondents of all malls, majority were regularly purchasing Grocery, Food, Cosmetics and cloths whereas they were purchasing other listed products occasionally or never.

Problems facing by respondents from selected cities

H_0 : Problems faced by respondents is significantly different in selected cities

Problem face	City				Total
	Ahmedabad	Rajkot	Surat	Vadodara	
High Price	27	19	25	14	85
	45.0%	31.7%	41.7%	23.3%	35.4%
Bad Product Quality	8	6	4	10	28
	13.3%	10.0%	6.7%	16.7%	11.7%
Far from the Home	22	27	23	33	105
	36.7%	45.0%	38.3%	55.0%	43.8%
Bad Service Quality	3	8	8	3	22
	5.0%	13.3%	13.3%	5.0%	9.2%
Total	60	60	60	60	240
	100.0%	100.0%	100.0%	100.0%	100.0%

Chi-Square Test			
Pearson Chi-Square	Value	df	Asymp. Sig. (2-sided)
	15.180	9	0.086

Problems facing by respondents from selected malls

H_0 : Problems faced by respondents is significantly different in selected malls

Problem Face	Malls								Total
	BC	BB	DM	Him	ISC	MO	Rel	SS	
High	2	30	13	5	9	6	14	6	85

Price	13.3%	40.0%	46.4%	31.2%	40.9%	26.1%	35.9%	27.3%	35.4%
Bad	3	4	5	3	1	1	5	6	28
Product Quality	20.0%	5.3%	17.9%	18.8%	4.5%	4.3%	12.8%	27.3%	11.7%
Far	9	31	8	8	8	15	17	9	105
from the Home	60.0%	41.3%	28.6%	50.0%	36.4%	65.2%	43.6%	40.9%	43.8%
Bad	1	10	2	0	4	1	3	1	22
Service Quality	6.7%	13.3%	7.1%	.0%	18.2%	4.3%	7.7%	4.5%	9.2%
Total	15	75	28	16	22	23	39	22	240
	100%	100%	100.0%	100.0%	100.0%	100.0%	100.0%	100.0%	100.0%

Chi-Square Test			
Pearson Chi-Square	Value	df	Asymp. Sig. (2-sided)
	28.057	21	0.139

Above table depicts that from selected 240 respondents, 85(35.4%) faced problem of high price, 28(11.7%) faced problem of bad product quality, 105(43.8%) faced problem of long distance whereas 22(9.2%) faced problem of bad service at mall. Majority of the respondents from D-Mart and IsconMalls faced problem of high price whereas majority of respondents from other malls faced problem of long distance of mall from their home. To check above hypothesis, statistical test named Chi-square was applied and obtained its p-value. Here, Chi – square value is 28.057 with p-vlaue 0.139. As p-value is more than 0.05, above null hypothesis is accepted and concluded that respondents from all malls faced almost same problems.

Overall Satisfaction of respondents from selected cities

H_0 : Overall Satisfaction of respondents is significantly different in selected cities

Overall Satisfaction level	City				Total
	Ahmedabad	Rajkot	Surat	Vadodara	
Highly Satisfied	7	19	17	20	63
	11.7%	31.7%	28.3%	33.3%	26.2%
Satisfied	38	17	20	15	90

	63.3%	28.3%	33.3%	25.0%	37.5%
Dissatisfied	10	20	16	18	64
	16.7%	33.3%	26.7%	30.0%	26.7%
Highly Dissatisfied	5	4	7	7	23
	8.3%	6.7%	11.7%	11.7%	9.6%
Total	60	60	60	60	240
	100.0%	100.0%	100.0%	100.0%	100.0%

Chi-Square Test			
	Value	df	Asymp. Sig. (2-sided)
Pearson Chi-Square	26.252	9	0.002

Above table depicts that from selected 240 respondents, 63(26.2%) were highly satisfied, 90(37.5%) were satisfied, 64(26.7%) were dissatisfied whereas 23(9.6%) were highly dissatisfied with the malls. Majority of the respondents from Ahmedabad were highly satisfied whereas respondents from other cities had mixed views regarding their satisfaction level in the malls. To check above hypothesis, statistical test named Chi-square was applied and obtained its p-value. Here, Chi – square value is 26.252 with p-vlaue 0.002. As p-value is less than 0.05, above null hypothesis is rejected and concluded that satisfaction level of respondents from selected cities is statistically significant.

Overall satisfaction of respondents from selected malls

H_0: Overall satisfaction of respondents is significantly different in selected malls

Overall Satisfaction	Malls								Total
	BC	BB	DM	Him	Isc	MO	Rel	SS	
Highly Satisfied	1	14	8	3	5	6	13	13	63
	6.7%	18.7%	28.6%	18.8%	22.7%	26.1%	33.3%	59.1%	26.2%
Satisfied	6	43	7	8	10	5	7	4	90
	40.0%	57.3%	25.0%	50.0%	45.5%	21.7%	17.9%	18.2%	37.5%
Dissatisfied	6	14	10	3	4	8	15	4	64
	40.0%	18.7%	35.7%	18.8%	18.2%	34.8%	38.5%	18.2%	26.7%
Highly Dissatisfied	2	4	3	2	3	4	4	1	23
	13.3%	5.3%	10.7%	12.5%	13.6%	17.4%	10.3%	4.5%	9.6%
Total	15	75	28	16	22	23	39	22	240
	100.0%	100.0%	100.0%	100.0%	100.0%	100.0%	100.0%	100.0%	100.0%

Chi-Square Test			
Pearson Chi-Square	Value	Df	Asymp. Sig. (2-sided)
	43.989	21	.002

Above table depicts that from selected 240 respondents, 63(26.2%) were highly satisfied, 90(37.5%) were satisfied, 64(26.7%) were dissatisfied whereas 23(9.6%) were highly dissatisfied with the malls. Majority of the respondents from Big Bazaar, MORE and Reliance Malls were dissatisfied whereas majority of respondents from Seven Seas were highly satisfied and respondents from other malls had mixed views regarding their satisfaction level. To check above hypothesis, statistical test named Chi-square was applied and obtained its p-value. Here, Chi – square value is 43.989 with p-vlaue 0.002. As p-value is less than 0.05, above null hypothesis is rejected and concluded that satisfaction level of respondents from selected malls is statistically significant.

Overall experience of respondents in malls from selected cities

H_0 : Overall experience of respondents in malls is significantly different in selected cities

Overall Experience	City				Total
	Ahmedabad	Rajkot	Surat	Vadodara	
Excellent	14	21	22	24	81
	23.3%	35.0%	36.7%	40.0%	33.8%
Good	31	14	16	20	81
	51.7%	23.3%	26.7%	33.3%	33.8%
Fair	11	20	17	12	60
	18.3%	33.3%	28.3%	20.0%	25.0%
Poor	4	5	5	4	18
	6.7%	8.3%	8.3%	6.7%	7.5%
Total	**60**	**60**	**60**	**60**	**240**
	100.0%	**100.0%**	**100.0%**	**100.0%**	**100.0%**

Chi-Square Test			
Pearson Chi-Square	Value	df	Asymp. Sig. (2-sided)
	15.156	9	.087

Above table says that from selected 240 respondents, 81(33.8%) had excellent experience, 81(33.8%) had good experience, 60(25.0%) had fair whereas 18(7.5%) had poor experience in the malls. Majority of the respondents from Ahmedabad had good experience whereas respondents from other cities had mixed views regarding their overall experience in malls. To check above hypothesis, statistical test named Chi-square was applied and obtained its p-value. Here, Chi – square value is 15.156 with p-value 0.087. As p-value is more than 0.05, above null hypothesis is accepted and concluded that overall experience of respondents from selected cities is almost same.

Overall experience of respondents in selected malls

H_0 : Overall experience of respondents is significantly different in selected malls

Overall	Malls								Total
Experience	BC	BB	DM	Him	Isc	MO	Rel	SS	
Excellent	1	15	11	7	7	9	17	14	81
	6.7%	20.0%	39.3%	43.8%	31.8%	39.1%	43.6%	63.6%	33.8%
Good	6	37	5	5	8	8	6	6	81

	40.0%	49.3%	17.9%	31.2%	36.4%	34.8%	15.4%	27.3%	33.8%
Fair	6	19	11	2	4	4	12	2	60
	40.0%	25.3%	39.3%	12.5%	18.2%	17.4%	30.8%	9.1%	25.0%
Poor	2	4	1	2	3	2	4	0	18
	13.3%	5.3%	3.6%	12.5%	13.6%	8.7%	10.3%	.0%	7.5%
Total	15	75	28	16	22	23	39	22	240
	100.0%	100.0%	100.0%	100.0%	100.0%	100.0%	100.0%	100.0%	100.0%

Chi-Square Test			
Pearson Chi-Square	Value	df	Asymp. Sig. (2-sided)
	41.051	21	0.006

Above table shows that from selected 240 respondents, 81(33.8%) had excellent and good experience in the malls whereas 60(25.0%) and 18(7.5%) had respectively fair and poor experience in the malls. Majority of the respondents had poor experience in Baroda Central, Himalaya, Iscon and Reliance Malls whereas majority of respondents from Seven Seas had either excellent or good experience. Respondents had mixed experience in other malls. To check above hypothesis, statistical test named Chi-square was applied and obtained its p-value. Here, Chi – square value is 41.051 with p-value 0.006. As p-value is less than 0.05, above null hypothesis is rejected and concluded that experience of respondents in selected malls is statistically significant.

Cross Tables

Distribution of respondents according to their overall service satisfaction and gender

H_0 : There is no significant association between overall service satisfaction and gender of respondents

Overall Service Satisfaction	Gender		Total
	Male	Female	
Highly Satisfied	49	14	63
	28.2%	21.2%	26.2%
Satisfied	66	24	90
	37.9%	36.4%	37.5%

Dissatisfied	43	21	64
	24.7%	31.8%	26.7%
Highly	16	7	23
Dissatisfied	9.2%	10.6%	9.6%
Total	174	66	240
	100.0%	100.0%	100.0%

Chi-Square Test			
	Value	df	Asymp. Sig. (2-sided)
Pearson Chi-Square	1.917	3	0.590

The table and graph provides distribution of respondents according to their overall service satisfaction and gender. Out of 240 respondents about 60% were satisfied with the services provided by different malls. Out of satisfied respondents, majority were male. To check the association between satisfaction level and gender of respondents, researcher had applied Chi-square test and obtained its p-value. Chi-square value is 1.917 with p-value 0.590. As p-value is more than 0.05, null hypothesis is accepted and concluded that there is no significant association between overall service satisfaction and gender of respondents.

Distribution of respondents according to their overall service satisfaction and monthly income

H_0 : There is no significant association between overall service satisfaction and monthly income of respondents

Overall Service Satisfaction	Income (Rs.)					Total
	<2500	2501-5000	5001-10000	10001-15000	>15000	
Highly Satisfied	10	30	10	5	8	63
	40.0%	37.5%	16.4%	16.7%	18.2%	26.2%
Satisfied	4	16	27	17	26	90
	16.0%	20.0%	44.3%	56.7%	59.1%	37.5%
Dissatisfied	8	28	18	5	5	64
	32.0%	35.0%	29.5%	16.7%	11.4%	26.7%
Highly Dissatisfied	3	6	6	3	5	23
	12.0%	7.5%	9.8%	10.0%	11.4%	9.6%

Total	25	80	61	30	44	240
	100 %	100 %	100 %	100 %	100 %	100 %

Chi-Square Test			
Pearson Chi-Square	Value	df	Asymp. Sig. (2-sided)
	37.017	12	0.000.

The table provides distribution of respondents according to their overall service satisfaction and monthly income. Out of 240 respondents more than 60% were satisfied with the services provided by different malls. Out of more satisfied respondents, majority were lower income group. To check the association between satisfaction level and monthly income of respondents, researcher had applied Chi-square test and obtained its p-value. Chi-square value is 37.017 with p-value 0.000. As p-value is less than 0.05, null hypothesis is rejected and concluded that there is significant association between overall service satisfaction and monthly income of respondents. Overall lower income group were more satisfied as compared to high income group.

Distribution of respondents according to their overall service satisfaction and marital status

H_0 : There is no significant association between overall service satisfaction and marital status of respondents

Overall Service Satisfaction	Marital Status				Total
	Married	Unmarried	Widow	Separated	
Highly satisfied	32	19	2	10	63
	34.8%	17.6%	16.7%	35.7%	26.2%
Satisfied	23	58	2	7	90
	25.0%	53.7%	16.7%	25.0%	37.5%
Dissatisfied	29	22	5	8	64
	31.5%	20.4%	41.7%	28.6%	26.7%
Highly Dissatisfied	8	9	3	3	23
	8.7%	8.3%	25.0%	10.7%	9.6%
Total	92	108	12	28	240

	100.0%	100.0%	100.0%	100.0%	100.0%

Chi-Square Test			
Pearson Chi-Square	Value	df	Asymp. Sig. (2-sided)
	27.696	9	0.001

The table provides distribution of respondents according to their overall service satisfaction and marital status. About 60% respondents were satisfied with the services provided by different malls. Majority of married respondents were highly satisfied whereas unmarried were not fully satisfied with the services of the malls. To check the association between satisfaction level and marital status of respondents, researcher had applied Chi-square test and obtained its p-value. Chi-square value is 27.696 with p-value 0.001. As p-value is less than 0.05, null hypothesis is rejected and concluded that there is significant association between overall service satisfaction and marital status of respondents.

Distribution of respondents according to their overall experience and monthly income

H_0 : There is no significant association between overall experience and monthly income of respondents

Overall Experience	Income (Rs.)					Total
	<2500	2501-5000	5001-10000	10001-15000	>15000	
Excellent	10	31	17	11	12	81
	40.0%	38.8%	27.9%	36.7%	27.3%	33.8%
Good	7	16	21	15	22	81
	28.0%	20.0%	34.4%	50.0%	50.0%	33.8%
Fair	5	29	17	3	6	60
	20.0%	36.2%	27.9%	10.0%	13.6%	25.0%
Poor	3	4	6	1	4	18
	12.0%	5.0%	9.8%	3.3%	9.1%	7.5%
Total	25	80	61	30	44	240
	100.0%	100.0%	100.0%	100.0%	100.0%	100.0%

Chi-Square Test			
Pearson Chi-Square	Value	df	Asymp. Sig. (2-sided)
	24.756	12	0.016

The table provides distribution of respondents according to their overall experience and monthly income. Out of 240 respondents more than 60% had good experience with the malls. Out of these respondents, majority were from higher income group. To check the association between experience and monthly income of respondents, researcher had applied Chi-square test and obtained its p-value. Chi-square value is 24.756 with p-value 0.016. As p-value is less than 0.05, null hypothesis is rejected and concluded that there is significant association between overall experience and monthly income of respondents.

H_0 : Mean value of service satisfaction grades in selected cities does not different significantly

H_1 : Mean value of service satisfaction grades in selected cities does different significantly

Overall Service Satisfaction of Consumers

City		Overall Service Satisfaction
Ahmedabad	Mean	2.22
	Std. Deviation	.761
Rajkot	Mean	2.15
	Std. Deviation	.954
Surat	Mean	2.22
	Std. Deviation	.993
Vadodara	Mean	2.20
	Std. Deviation	1.038
Total	Mean	2.20
	Std. Deviation	.937

ANOVA Table

Source of variation	Sum of Squares	df	Mean Square	F	p-value
Between Groups	.179	3	.060	.067	.977
Within Groups	209.617	236	.888	-	-
Total	209.796	239	-	-	-

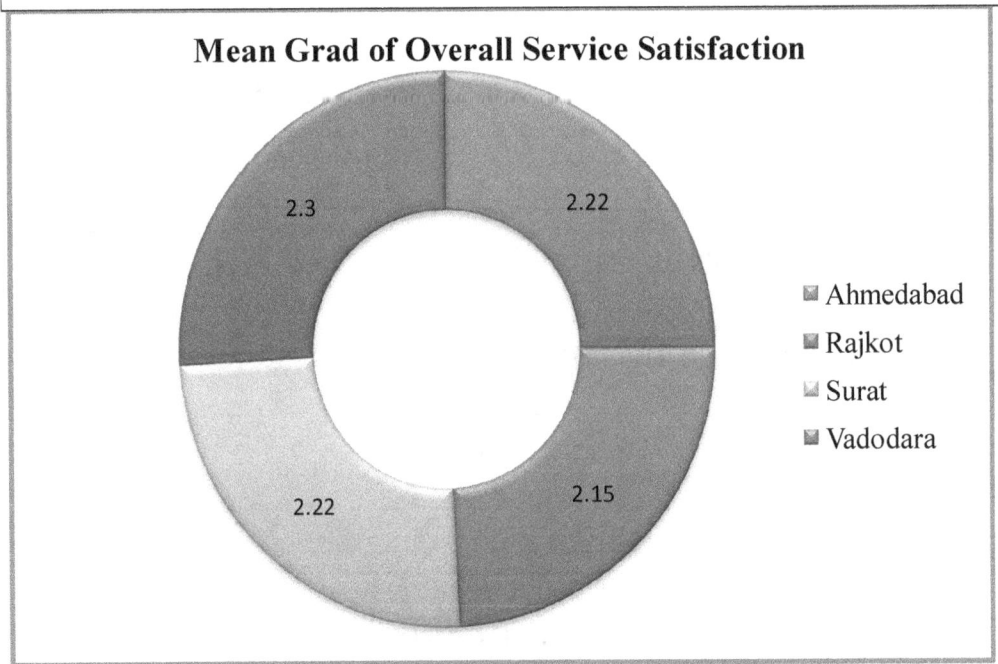

Mean Grad of Overall Service Satisfaction

2.3 — 2.22 — 2.22 — 2.15

- Ahmedabad
- Rajkot
- Surat
- Vadodara

Overall Service Satisfaction of Consumers

Above table depicts Overall service satisfaction of Consumers during study period (according to selected respondents). It shows overall service satisfaction grade 2.20, i.e. good experience was shown.

To compare difference in mean grades between

selected cities, ANOVA test was used and F & P – values were obtained. As shown in above ANOVA table, p-value was more than 5%. Hence it can be concluded that the mean value of service satisfaction grades in selected cities was not significantly different. It means overall service satisfaction was on an average level in all cities.

CHAPTER-6

FINDINGS, SUGGESTIONS, CONCLUSION

This chapter discusses findings, suggestions and conclusion for the present study. They are based on details of data analysis with respect to theoretical concept based on the primary data collected from selected cities of Gujarat based shopping malls.

Findings are nothing else but the summarized interpretation of the data that is collected and analyzed. If one wants to know what a particular research says, one should just go through the findings. That can be reached by analyzing all the data collected viz. primary and secondary.

While discussing with consumers and management of shopping Malls, Consumers and management of shopping malls were interviewed and requested to answer the questionnaire. They were contacted personally to avoid misunderstanding. On the basis of data analysis and interpretation many findings were found, the findings are as follows:

FINDINGS:

- From Vadodara, "Baroda Centre", "MORE" and "Seven Seas" malls were selected. "Big Bazaar", "Himalaya" and "Reliance" malls were selected from Ahmedabad. From Rajkot and Surat cities, "Big Bazaar", "D-Mart", "Iscon" and "Reliance" malls were selected for the present study. Alost equal proportions of respondents were taken from each city. The age distribution of respondents was also equally distributed.

- There were about 70% male and 30% female respondents in the study. Majority of the respondents were students and self employed persons. Among selected respondents majority had average monthly income between Rs. 2501-5000/-. In this study very few respondents were having low level education (SSC or low).

- In this study 45% respondents were unmarried, 38% married and rest were either widow or separated.

- Among selected respondents, 32.1% were higher

educated, 25.8% were graduate, 28.7% had passed up to HSC level, 8.3% had passed up to SSC level whereas only 5% were uneducated.

- From selected respondents, about 20% were visiting malls more than five times a week whereas about10% were visiting once a week and 30% were visiting occasionally. Majority of respondents were visiting malls in the evening. House wives and students were visiting malls in either morning or afternoon. More than 70% respondents preferred week-ends to visit a mall.

- As far as time spent in mall is concerned, students and house wives spent more time in malls as compared to service persons or self employed persons. Students got information regarding malls from their friends, advertisements and internet whereas house wives got the details from neighbors, relatives and friends.

- Service people and self employed persons got the details from news paper, advertisements, internet and colleagues / friends. There were very small group of respondents who said that they got information regarding malls from dealers.

- About 30% respondents take self-decision regarding selection of malls whereas rest of all are dependents on others. As per majority of respondents, Store atmosphere, good elevator system, easily accessible billing Nears, Trail rooms and Promotion schemes are very important facilities for every malls. Grocery, Food items and Cosmetics were regularly purchased by respondents.

- The distance of mall from home, high price of items, bad product quality and service, advertisement and few promotional schemes are major problems faced by respondents.

- In Vadodara and Rajkot, distance of malls from home was a major problem. Respondents from Ahmedabad and Surat were more unsatisfied with the price of items whereas those from Vadodara were quite satisfied with the price.

- As per all respondents, Store atmosphere, good

elevator system, Easily accessible billing Nears, Ample parking space are very important for any mall whereas Promotion schemes, Trail rooms, Convenient layout are some essential things which should be in a mall.

- Food, Entertainment, Cosmetics, Grocery items were regularly purchased by respondents from the malls.

- Major problems faced by respondents of Ahmedabad and Surat were high price of items in malls whereas major problem of Rajkot and Vadodara respondents was distance of malls from their home. Some other problems like bad service and product in malls were faced by customers of malls. Overall there is no significant difference in problems faced by respondents from different cities.

- There is significant difference in satisfaction level of respondents from various cities. Respondents from Vadodara city were more satisfied followed by Rajkot, Surat and Ahmedabad. Despite of various services and attractive offers served by malls, more than 30% of respondents were not satisfied with the malls in their cities. Respondents from Ahmedabad were unsatisfied with mall services.

- Among satisfied respondents, majority were customers of Big – Bazaar, Reliance and Seven – Seas Malls. There is significant difference in dissatisfaction of respondents from various malls.

- A small group (8%) of respondents was not satisfied with mall services and hence they said that they had poor experience with the malls in their cities whereas as per 25% of respondents the experience with the malls was fair. There was a large group of respondents (65%) who said that they had excellent/good experience with the malls. Overall there is no significant difference in experience with malls between respondents from selected cities.

- Majority of respondents from Baroda Central, Himalaya, Reliance and Iscon mall had bad experience whereas Seven Sease, Big Bazaar and D-

Mart customers had good experience with the malls. There is significant difference in experience at malls between customers from selected malls.

- About 60% of respondents had good experience in malls. As far as satisfaction is concerned, male respondents were more satisfied than female. But the difference in satisfaction level between male and female respondents was not statistically significant.

- Overall service satisfaction of respondents is very much affected by their income. Respondents having low monthly income were more satisfied as compared to those having higher package of income.

- Satisfaction level of Widow / Separated respondents was lower as compared to married or unmarried respondents. Marital status is significantly affected to overall service satisfaction. Married respondents were more satisfied than unmarried one.

- There is significant role of education on overall

service satisfaction level of respondents. Respondents with low / no education were more satisfied as compared to higher educated respondents.

- Respondent's age significantly affects satisfaction level. Students and 50+ aged respondents were less satisfied as compared to middle aged group.

- Students and house wives were less satisfied as compared to professionals and self employed. Thus occupation had significant role on service satisfaction in malls.

- Expenditure (in the malls) of respondents having age between 25-35 yrs was higher than other respondents. As far as gender is concerned, expenditure capacity of males was higher than females.

- Respondents with young age (specially students) were more frequently visiting malls as compared to others. Male respondents were visiting malls more frequently than females.

- As far as time spent in mall is concerned, Students

spent more time in malls followed by respondents aged >35 yrs. There is no difference in average time spent by male and female respondents in the mall.

- It was found that all shopping malls are interested in providing better services to customers.

- All major services are very important to provide to customers by shopping malls.

- Most of information is supplied to consumers through television, newspaper, hoardings, and their own announcement systems.

- Most of consumers prefer evening and some consumers are interested to visit the mall in morning and afternoon.

- Most of consumers are interested in Sunday and Wednesday for visiting the Malls.

- It was observed that most of consumers (100%) spend more than 30 minutes in the Malls.

- Food is demanded regularly and electronics and home décor are demanded sometimes in the Malls by consumers.

- All shopping malls are thinking towards providing better services to consumers.

- Most of consumers visit the Malls.

- Overall service satisfaction was on an average level in all cities.

SUGGESTIONS:

On the basis of many findings, there are many suggestions needed to improve the management of Malls, the suggestions are as follows:

- Malls do supply most of information to consumers about offers through newspapers, hoardings.

- Managers of the malls should take some initiatives to get feedback from the customers visiting the mall.

- Management of malls should provide customer-friendly environment in the malls.

- Management of Malls should think towards providing better services to consumer and improving the retail market.

- There should be continuous research and development for the development of the Mall.

- Keeping in the mind the requirements of customers with different age, education and occupation; management should provide all items with a attractive rates / scheme.

- Environment and overall service of the mall should be to the mark of satisfaction for the customers.

- Managers of the mall also think over the area / site for the mall, so that it can be easily accessible and reachable for the customers.

- Management of the mall should provide enough space for parking.

- The sign boards kept on the items for the various scheme and price should be clear and easily accessible for the customers.

- Retailers should keep themselves and the units updated with the latest product in the market to retain their consumers.

- Mass media like television, newspapers etc. are to be extensively used for the purpose of publicity.

- A store should have an inviting appearance that makes the customer feel comfortable and yet eager to buy.

- Innovation in the organization, financing and delivery of community service.

- Greater effort must be spent on merchandise displays that make it easier for the customer to find and purchase the items they want or need.

- Good prices and positive word of mouth advertising is important.

- Special emphasis should be placed on the store's window displays because they are the information link to the potential customer.

- Selling space is the most important part of a store and therefore, efforts to utilize each square foot will help to maximize sales.

- The main principles of design used in display are balance, emphasis, proportion, rhythm, colour, lighting and harmony.

- An effective way of attracting customers to a store is by having good displays, both exterior and interior.

- The customer has to keep himself always updated with the latest development in the retail industry so that he can reap the maximum benefits offered by the retailers.

- Consumers can restrict their purchases within their budget for provisions.

- Nowadays, various services are provided by retailer, the customer can derive the maximum benefits and comforts from his purchase.

- The customer may check the authenticity in schemes and may calculate real benefit.

- Customers should update themselves regarding various promotion schemes given by the malls.

- Customers should collect all information from various malls in their area / city and compare the price, quality, company/brand and service provided by the malls.

- On the basis of the knowledge taken by comparison of services of malls, last decision on selecting malls for purchasing items should be taken.

- Customers should give their feedback and suggestions to the authorities of the malls for better service.

- Finally, customer's satisfaction regarding quality of items and management's satisfaction regarding their business progress should be simultaneously served.

CONCLUSION:

From the present study researcher found that overall experience of the respondents regarding selected malls is good. Though many facilities are provided by Malls to consumers, customer preferred relaxation and enjoyment, more space to move in a good elevator system, convenient layout at the Malls, easily accessible billing counters and easily locatable stairs, prolonged experience.

The major problems faced by respondents were the distance of mall from home and high price of items. Other problems were quality of service and less promotional activities. Respondents from Ahmedabad and Surat were unsatisfied by price of items in the malls. Respondents from Vadodara city were more satisfied followed by Rajkot, Surat and Ahmedabad. Among satisfied respondents, majority were customers of Big – Bazaar, Reliance and Seven – Seas Malls.

Retailing has now become one of the leading industries that is adding a lot to the GDP of our country. This is thereby helping the nation to develop and has given employment opportunities to many skilled as well as unskilled people. Therefore the government has to provide enough support to all those retail chain stores so that the country would develop further.

Customer satisfaction has now become one of the major key factors for every entrepreneur to carry out his business. Retailing is one such form of business where they target on customer satisfaction by making all possible arrangements for them to come and shop in comfort.

Bibliography

- **Books**
  - Bansal S.P, Verma O.P., Marketing Research, Ludhiana, Kalyani Publishers, First Edition, 2007.
  - Berman Barry and Evans, R. Joel, Retail Management: A Strategic Approach, New Delhi, Pearson Eduction Asia, Eight Edition, 2002.
  - Bose Biplab S., Marketing Management [Taxes & Cases] Mumbai, Himalaya Publishing, House, First Edition, 2007.
  - C.B. Dasadia (JIC & GM), An Industrial Outline of Ahmedabad District, District Industries Centrel, BachatBhavan, Ahmedabad 1 (2005)
  - Chunawalla S.A, Commentary on Consumer Behavior, Mumbai, Himalaya Publishing House, Millennium, Reprint Edition, 2001.
  - Chunawalla S.A., Contours of Retailing Management, Mumbai, Himalaya Publishing House, First Edition, 2006.

- Chunawalla S.A., Marketing Principles and Practices, Mumbai, Himalaya Publishing House, Second Edition, 2006.

- Davat R.S., Modern Marketing Management

- Desai S.S.M., Industrial Economy of India, Himalaya Publishing House, Mumbai, First Edition, 1988

- Desai Vasant, Dynamics of Entrepreneurial Development and Management, Humalaya Publishing House, Mumbai Reprint (June 2002)

- Desai Vasant, Indian Industry, Himalaya Publishing House, Mumbai First Edition, 1987

- Dhotre, Meenal, Channel Management and Retail Marketing, Mumbai, Himalaya Publishing House, First Edition, 2005.

- Economic Survey, Oxford University Press, Government of India, Ministry of Finance, Economic Division, New Delhi 1, 2003-04, 2006-07, 2007-08

- Francis Cherunilam, Business Environment: Texts and Cases, Himalaya Publishing House, Juy 2003

- Gupta R.S.,Sharma B.D., Bhalla N.S., Principles and Practice of Management, Kalyani Publishers, Ludhiana, Reprint, 2000

- Hill Richard M., Alexander Ralpsh S., Cross James S., Industrial Marketing, All India Travellers Booksellers, Delhi, 1986

- Hirway Indira, Dynamics of Development in Gujarat: some Issues, Centre for Development Alternatives, Bodakdev, Ahmedabad 15

- Industries Commissionerate, Industries in Gujarat: Some Statistics, Gujarat State, Gandhinagar, 1999-2000, 2004, 2007

- Industries, Gujarat 2006-2007, Infomedia Yellow Pages, Mumbai 400 028

- Kothari C.R., Research Methodology Methods and Techniques, New Delhi, WishwaPrakashan, Second Edition.

- Kotler Philip and Armstrong, Principles of Marketing, Prentice Hall of India Private Limited, New Delhi, Ninth Edition, 2001

- Kotler Philip, Marketing Management, Delhi, Pearson Education Pvt. Ltd., Eleventh Edition, 2003.

- Kumar Arun, Sharma Rachana, Marketing Management, Atlantic Publishers, New Delhi, 1998

- Levy, Michad and Weitz A barton, Retailing Management, New Delhi, Tata McGraw-Hill Publishing Co. Ltd., Fifth Edition, 2003.

- MalhotraNaresh K., Marketing Research- An applied Orientation, New Delhi, Prentice-Hall of India Pvt. Ltd., Fourth Edition, 2005.

- Nair Suja R., Consumer Behavior and Marketing Research, Mumbai, Himalaya Publishing House, Forth Edition, 2007.

- Nair Suja, Retail Management, Mumbai, Himalaya Publishing House, First Edition, 2006.

- Ramaswamy V.S., Namakumari S., Marketing Management, New Delhi, McMillan India Pvt. Ltd., Third Edition, 2002.

- Rana T.J., Editor, Business Organisation and Management, SudhirPrakashan, Ahmedabad, Twenty Second Edition, 2007-2008

- RathodRaju M., Encouraging Stories of Successful Entrepreneurs, Sardar Patel University (50th Golden Jubilee), VallabhVidyanagar (15 December, 2004)

- Schiffman Leon G. and Kanuk Leslie Lazar, Consumer Behavior, New Delhi, Prentice-Hall of India Pvt. Ltd., Sixth Edition, 2001.

- Shah P.M., Business Organisation and Management, Kumar Prakashan, Ahmedabad, Latest Edition 2008-2009.

- Shah A.D., " A study of consumer behavior in Malls vis-à-vis Mom & Pop Shops, Thesis, September 2009.

- Sherlekar S.A., Marketing Management, Mumbai, Himalaya Publishing House, Reprint-2002.

- Sherlekar S.A., Sherlekar V.S., Modern Business Organisation and Management, Himalaya Publishing House, Mumbai, Reprint, 1992

- Sonatakki C.N., Principle of Marketing, Ludhiana, Kalyani Publishers, First Edition, 2000.

- Sontakki C.N., Marketing Management, Mumbai, Himalaya Publishing House, First Edition, 2006.

- Vedmani Gibson G., Retail Management functional Principles & Practices, Mumbai, Jaico Publishing House, Second Edition, Revised & Enlarged, 2004.

■ **Magazines and Journals**

- 4PS Business and Marketing, Vol.-2, issue 11, 6 July-19 July, 2007.

- Business India, November 18, 2007.

- Business Today, Fortnightly Magazine, December 16, 2007.

- IBEF, Bennett, Coleman & Co. Ltd., 2007

- Indian Journal of Marketing, Volume -37, No. 10, October-2007.

- Indian Journal of Marketing, Volume -37, No. 11, November-2007.

- Indian Journal of Marketing, Volume -37, No. 3, March-2005.

- Indian Journal of Marketing, Volume -37, No. 3, March-2007.

- Indian Journal of Marketing, Volume -37, No. 4, April-2006.

- Indian Journal of Marketing, Volume -37, No. 8, August-2007.

- Indian Management Vol.-44, issue 6, June 2005.

- Retail, Vol. 7, No.1, January, 2008.

- Retail, Vol.-6, No.9, September, 2007.

- Retailer, India Edition, Vol. -2, No. 4, 15th August – 30th September, 2007.

- Retailer, India Edition, Vol. -2, No. 5, October, 2007.

- Retailer, India Edition, Vol. -2, No. 8, 15th January-14th February, 2008.

- Souvenir: International Conference on Management (INCOM 2008), Managing Global Business Competition (22-24 September, 2008), organised by MHRM Programme, Department of Business administration, MohanlalSukhadiya University, Udaipur, Raj. India.

- Synergy-I.T.S Journal of I.T. & Management, Volume-5, No. 2, July-2007.

- Synergy-I.T.S Journal of I.T.%& Management, Volume-5, No. 2, July-2007.

- The Drivers of Inclusive Economic Growth (Courtesy: NMIMS), Vol. II, No. 11, November, 2008, pp 162-166

- The ICFAI Journal of Management Research, Vol.-6, No.6, 2007.

- **Newspapers**

- Gujarat Samachar, Ahmedabad Plus, Friday, 05th August, 2011

- Gujarat Samachar, "Ravi Purti", Sunday, 18th December, 2011.

- Sandesh, Thursday, 22nd April 2010.

- The Economic Times, Sunday, 30th December, 2007.

- The Economic Times, Monday, 31st December, 2007.

- The Economic Times, Thursday, 14th February, 2008.

▪ Webliography

- http://en.wikipedia.org/wiki/Vadodara

- www.ahmedabadline.com

- www.economictimes.com

- www.enwikipedia.org

- www.google.com

- www.gujaratglobal.com

- www.imagesretail.com

- www.indiacatalog.com

- www.indianbusiness.nic.in

- www.indiaretailing.com
- www.ksatechnopak.com
- www.mapsofindia.com/maps/gujarat/ahmedabad city.htm
- www.retailindustry.com
- www.retailnews.com
- www.retailsector.co.in
- www.timesofindia.indiatimes.com
- www.walmart.com